The Civilization Library
Published in the United States by
Gloucester Press in 1979

Originated and designed by
Charles Matheson,
David Cook Associates,
produced by
The Archon Press Ltd
70 Old Compton Street
London W1V 5PA

First published in
Great Britain 1978 by
Hamish Hamilton
Children's Books Ltd
90 Great Russell Street
London WC1B 3PT

Printed in Italy

Dr. S. Hugh-Jones is a Lecturer in
Social Anthropology at Cambridge
University, and Fellow of Kings
College, Cambridge.
The publishers would like to
acknowledge the Dept. of
Ethnography at the British
Museum for providing access to
the Tayler/Moser collection.

Library of Congress Cataloging in Publication Data

Hugh-Jones, Stephen, 1945 —
  Amazonian Indians.

  (The Civilization library)
  Includes index.
  SUMMARY: Describes the Barasana Indians of the
Amazon River Basin and their life style which, due to
their isolated environment, is very much like that of
their ancestors.
  1. Barasana Indians – Juvenile literature.
  [1. Barasana Indians.   2. Indians of South America]
  I. Wilson, Maurice Charles John, 1914 –
  II. Title. III. Series.
  F2270.2.B27H823   1979   980' .004' 98   78–24568
  ISBN 0–531–01448–7

THE CIVILIZATION LIBRARY

AMAZONIAN INDIANS

Stephen Hugh-Jones

Illustrated by
Maurice Wilson

Gloucester Press · New York · 1979

The Barasana people

Barasana woman
The native peoples of South America originally came from Asia. Some Barasana faces show this Mongolian ancestry in slanted eyes and high cheekbones. In the past both men and women had long hair, but now men cut their hair short. Women wear their hair in small topknots. They may decorate their faces with black paint made from leaves. Red face paint is a sign of friendliness and wards off danger. Necklaces of small glass beads are valuable items of trade.

This book is about the ancient traditional way of life of the Vaupés Indians as represented by the Barasana. The Barasana are a small group living on the Pirá-Paraná River in South America. Their homeland lies near the equator on the border of Colombia and Brazil. The land is covered by thick tropical forest, an endless sea of green with bright patches of color made by the tops of flowering trees. Breaking through the trees like islands are steep-sided, flat-topped mountains.

The principal rivers of the region flow eastward to the mighty Amazon. They cut through the stony mountains, and are blocked by waterfalls and dangerous rapids.

In clearings on the river banks live some 15,000 Amazonian Indians who make their living by hunting, fishing, and farming. The Indians are divided into many small groups, each speaking its own language. Although they have different names, such as Tucano, Cubeo, Desana, and Barasana, they are not really independent tribes because they intermarry and share a common way of life that has changed very little over the centuries. Their languages all belong to the same family—Tucanoan.

The Barasana and their neighbors have been protected by isolation and the dangerous river from some of the worst effects of civilization. Their lives are still very much like those of their ancestors.

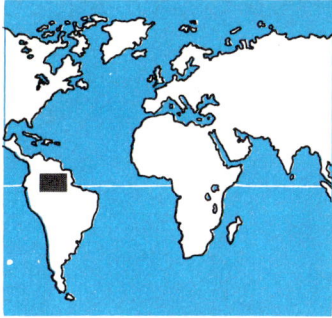

The Amazon Basin

The region around the Amazon River in South America is shown above. The map below shows the section near the Vaupés River, and some of the Indian groups located there.

Cubeo

Barasana

Pirá-Paraná R.

Vaupés R.

Desána

Tucano

(62 mi.)

0   (100 km.)

Amazon R.

A forest clearing

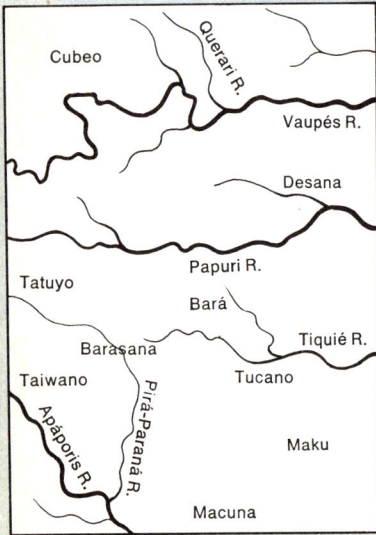

The Barasana have no villages; instead, small groups of people live in a *maloca*, or communal house. Each maloca is separated from its neighbors by about an hour's journey. The people visit each other often, however, attending dances and eventually intermarrying. Most malocas are built close to big rivers where the fishing is good and travel by canoe is easy.

Each maloca is surrounded by a cleared yard. Behind the house are small gardens for special plants—peppers, tobacco, and plants providing medicines and drugs. Banana trees bordering the yard provide fruit, and banana leaves are used for serving plates. In nearby clearings are larger gardens, or *chagras*. From the air, the clearings around the malocas look like light-green holes in the forest.

Vaupés Indian groups
Each group has a traditional territory. The Tatuyo live in the headwater region of the Pirá-Paraná, the Macuna near the river's mouth, the Barasana across the middle, with the Taiwano and Bará on either side.

There are about 300 Barasana Indians, and other groups are roughly the same size. The Indians believe that each group is descended from a huge anaconda, or water snake, who became a human being.

From five to thirty people live in each maloca. The men are usually brothers. The women are their wives and their unmarried sisters. Since Barasana people must marry partners from other Indian groups, married sisters move away to live with their husbands, who may be Tatuyo, Taiwano, Macuna, or Bará.

As the men grow older and their sons grow up and marry, the household becomes larger and larger. When the headman of the older generation dies, the house is abandoned. The people move together to a new site nearby.

Looking after the maloca

The palm leaf thatch of the maloca often needs patching. Men collect new leaves in the forest, bring them back to the maloca, and weave them onto strips of wood. The new sections of thatch are put in place from a scaffold inside the house. Malocas are made as large as possible to hold many visitors and leave room for dancing. Big malocas are called *basaria wi* ("dance houses"). Paths lead from the front door to the river, and from the back door to a stream and on to the gardens. Other paths lead to the forest and to neighboring malocas.

The maloca

A miniature universe

The maloca is a model of the Barasana world. The roof represents the sky and beams of light shining through small holes are the stars. The posts are mountains supporting the sky. The ridgepole is the path of the sun across the heavens. The front door, facing east, is the "door in the east" and the back door "the door in the west." An imaginary river, "the river of the dead," flows under the house. In the evening the sun sets in the west, going down into the river where it sails upstream until it rises in the east next morning. The dead are buried in the center of the house in coffins made from canoes. The maloca also represents a person; the ridgepole is his spine; the painted housefront is his face.

A maloca lasts for about fifteen years. To build a new one, which may be 100 feet (30 m) long, takes about a year. Most of the building is done by the men who will live in the house, but they may be helped by neighbors. The eldest brother usually directs the work and he will be the headman of the new maloca. A large maloca, with many people living in it, brings greater prestige to the headman.

After clearing the ground, a plan for the house, which always faces east, is drawn in the sand. Two rows of center posts are sunk deep in the earth, with smaller posts at the sides. The ridgepole at the top of the house rests on small poles lashed to the center beam running the length of the house. Other beams carry long, thin poles running down from the housetop almost to the ground. When the framework is completed, the men go to the forest for leaves, returning with heavy bundles on their backs. They weave the leaves into a thick thatch for the roof.

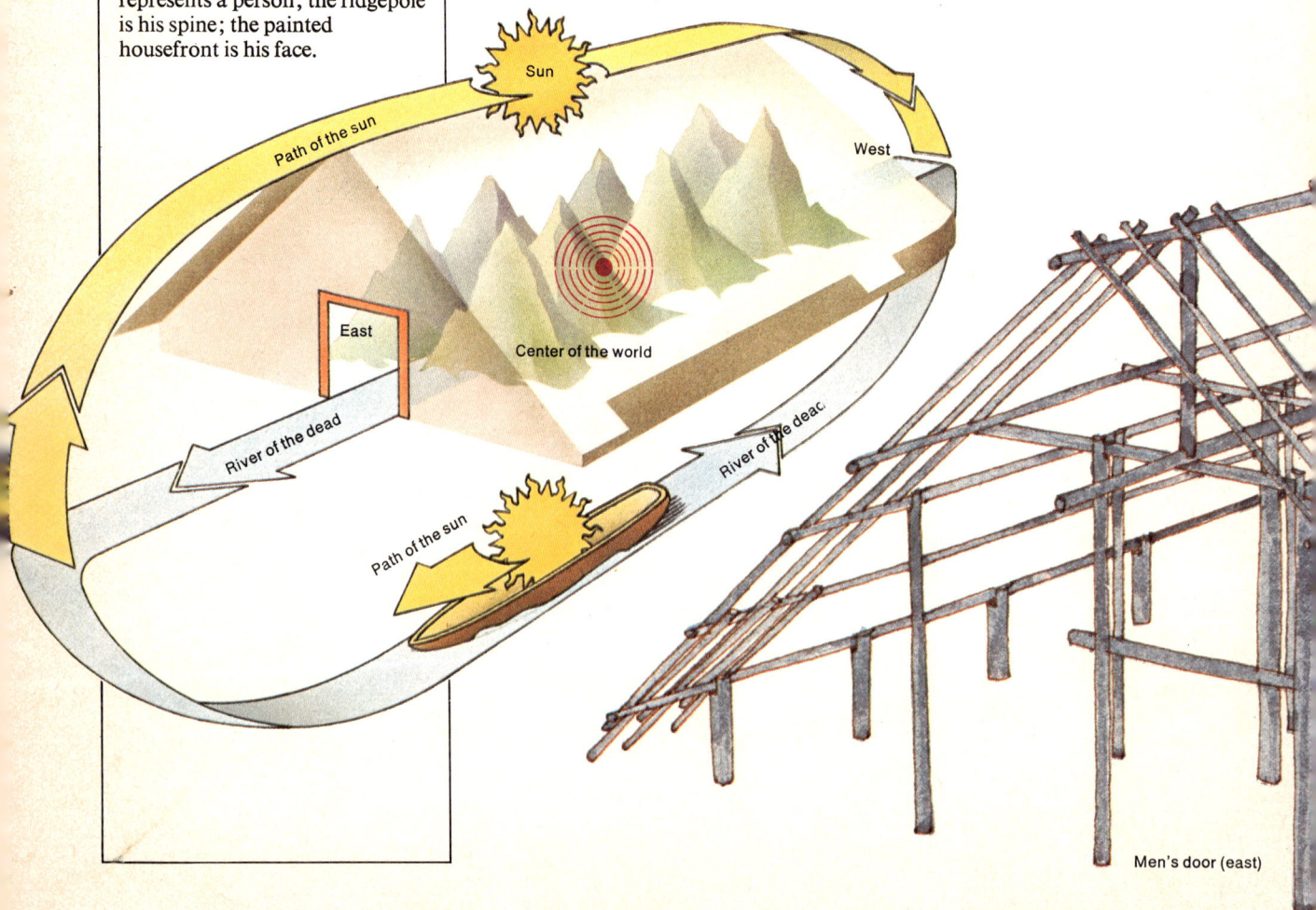

Sun

Path of the sun

West

East

Center of the world

River of the dead

River of the dead

Path of the sun

Men's door (east)

As soon as one section of the roof is finished, the people, who have been camping nearby, move into their new home. When all the work is finished and the front of the house has been painted, a big dance is held. It is attended by people from all the neighboring malocas. It celebrates the end of the work and rewards the people who helped. During the dance the shamans (who act as priests and doctors) chant and blow spells with smoke from big cigars to make the house strong, protect it from thunder and lightning, and keep the inhabitants safe.

The maloca serves as a family home, a workshop, a meeting place, a dance hall, and a place of worship. To the Barasana it also represents the whole universe. Every married man makes a screened-off compartment in the maloca where he will live with his wife and children. The back of the maloca serves as a kitchen. Unmarried men and guests sleep in the open area near the front.

Lashing
The framework of the maloca is lashed together with vines. Smoke spells are blown over the vines to keep them tight.

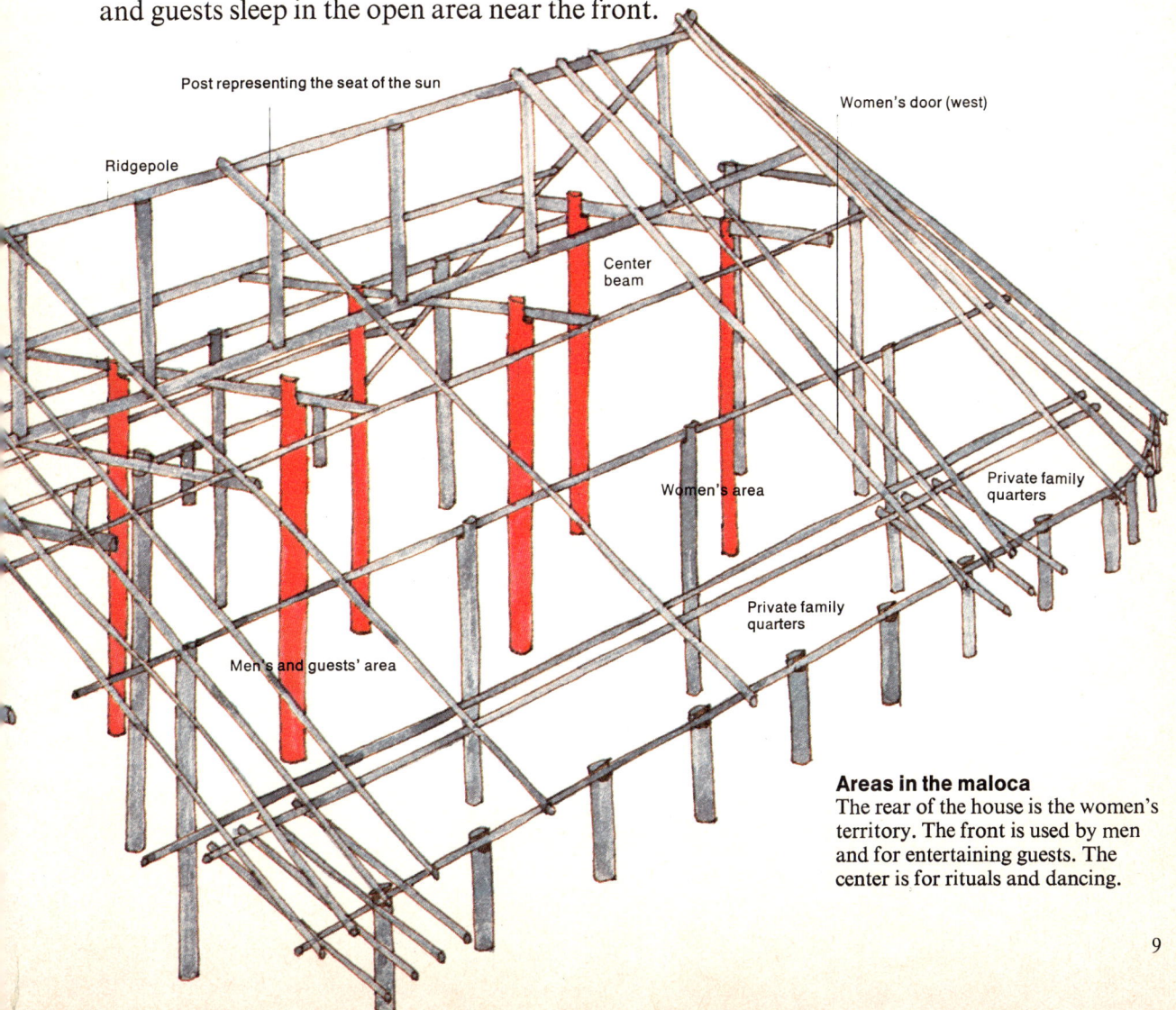

Post representing the seat of the sun

Women's door (west)

Ridgepole

Center beam

Women's area

Private family quarters

Private family quarters

Men's and guests' area

Areas in the maloca
The rear of the house is the women's territory. The front is used by men and for entertaining guests. The center is for rituals and dancing.

9

Inside

Life in the maloca

The Barasana get up very early and go to the river to bathe. Breakfast is a light meal—usually manioc bread dipped in a hot sauce. Men provide meat and fish for the family and women provide manioc (or cassava)—a root vegetable. After breakfast people go off to work. Women go to the chagras and men stay behind to work in the house, or go out to hunt or fish. Men and women make different things. Men weave baskets, carve stools and big troughs and make weapons and fishing gear. Men also grow the corn, which is stored in the rafters, and make the dance ornaments, which hang from the beams in palm leaf boxes. Women make pottery and body paint, sew clothes, weave hammocks, and do almost all of the cooking and farming. The women raise small animals and birds as pets (chickens are pets and are never eaten). Macaws are kept for their feathers. Their skins are rubbed with a special fruit, so the feathers grow bright orange and are used for feather crowns. Dusk is a time for family life—when the men play with their children. At night the men sit together telling stories, chewing coca, and smoking cigars. The women sit toward the back of the maloca. They go to bed in their hammocks earlier than the men do.

Farming the forest

To make their chagras, the Indians clear patches of forest near the maloca, burn the tree stumps, and plant their crops in the ashes. When the crops have been harvested, a chagra is abandoned and gradually turns back into forest. The forest cover gradually restores fertility to the soil so that after a few years the old site can be cleared and used again. This way of farming is called "slash and burn" and is used throughout the area.

Many crops are grown in one chagra; plants of different heights provide shade for one another and keep the soil from washing away in heavy rains. Crops like pineapples, tobacco, peanuts, and manioc are native plants. The Indians also grow bananas, sugarcane, and yams—which were brought in by Europeans. Canes for arrows, vines to make poisons, and leaves to make body paint and medicines are also raised.

The women do most of the farm work once the men have cleared the land. Every morning manioc is collected for the day's supply of bread. The women peel the heavy roots and load them into baskets, which are carried with the help of bark strips over the head.

Slash and burn
Men clear the undergrowth, fell trees, and later set fire to the dry branches and leaves. Women plant food crops in the ashes. Men raise special crops— coca, corn, poison vines, and yagé (from which a strong drink is made). The manioc is ready to harvest in about nine months, and produces edible roots for three years. After that, weeds take over the garden but coca and bananas continue to be harvested. A new chagra is cleared every year so that one is always ready to harvest.

1 Maloca
2 Clearing and burning the forest
3 Newly-planted chagra
4 Chagra ready to harvest
5 Chagra with encroaching jungle
6 Abandoned chagra with new forest growth

The women's world

The lives of Barasana men and women are sharply divided. They use different doors and carry out their separate tasks in different areas of the maloca. Outside, women work in the chagras and harvest the crops while men go hunting in the forest or fishing on the rivers.

The world of women revolves around the care of children, growing crops, and preparing food. Manioc is an important part of the diet and the work of turning it into food takes up much of their time. The leaves are eaten like spinach. Boiled manioc juice makes a drink (boiled longer, it becomes a caramel-flavored sauce). Bread is made from grated roots. Toasted bread, mixed with juice and fermented, makes a beer served at dances. *Farinha* is dried manioc, which keeps for a long time and can be carried on journeys. When they are busy preparing manioc, women put their babies in special swings hung from the roof to keep them safe from harm.

Women and children sometimes go off to the forest on expeditions called "looking and eating." They collect ants, frogs, and caterpillars, fish in streams for crabs and shrimp, and chop down fruit trees with axes. They eat as much as they can and bring the rest home. Families also go camping on river banks to catch fish or eat ripe fruit. Sometimes the whole household goes off to camp in shelters and gather food.

Pottery
To make pottery, women use clay from the banks of streams. The clay is mixed with ash to make it stronger. Pots are shaped from coils of clay. The sides are smoothed with a piece of gourd and later polished with a pebble. The pot is baked to harden it and then coated with leaf juice and smoked to give it a black glaze.

Preparing manioc
Manioc contains prussic acid, which must be removed before the manioc is safe to eat. Manioc roots (1) are grated on a board set with sharp stone chips (2) and the pulp is put in a sieve on a tripod (3). Water is poured over it, washing juice into a pot below. The juice is boiled to rid it of poison (4). Before the pulp is used for baking bread the rest of the acid is removed by putting the pulp in a *tipiti* (a long sack) hanging from a pole (5). A woman sits on another pole attached to the bottom of the tipiti (opposite page). Her weight squeezes it and forces the liquid out through the sides into a bowl below.

Life on the river

The Barasana and their neighbors are "river people." They live near rapids where fish are plentiful, and they travel by canoe. Much of their food comes from rivers. They believe that the first people came upriver from the east and they think of rivers as the source of life.

Some Barasana men specialize in making canoes. They are highly skilled and the canoes are valued trading items. Barasana are also expert boatmen and know of ways through the dangerous rapids that block the rivers. Large canoes are used for carrying people and goods over long distances, and small ones, just big enough for one person, for hunting and fishing. At night the Indians hunt from canoes, using torches and shooting at the eyes of animals reflected in the torchlight.

The Indians know where to find and how to catch each kind of fish. Fish are caught with hook and line, shot with bows and arrows, trapped, speared with harpoons, and even chopped in half with machetes as they swim by.

Shooting and trapping fish
Fish are shot with arrows which have hollow shafts that float. Or a river is dammed (below). Poisonous vines are trampled into the water, stunning the fish which are then trapped or speared.

Roe

Liké

Biri (catfish)

River fish
Fish are boiled with peppers or smoked on racks to dry and preserve them.

Making canoes
The Barasana do not make birchbark canoes like those of the North American Indians. Their canoes are dugouts made from the trunks of very large trees hollowed out and then heated over a fire to soften the wood. The sides are wedged apart with wooden pegs and kept open by the seats, which are forced into place. The charring of the fire keeps the wood from rotting.

Food from the forest

Although there are many different animals in the Amazon rain forest, they are hard to find. But the Indians know their habits well and are able to follow them by studying broken branches, fallen fruit, and tracks. They also lure animals and birds by imitating their calls.

Only men hunt and the best hunters are much admired. Although the Indians eat more fish than meat, Barasana men prefer hunting to fishing. Stories of past hunts and of animals they have recently seen dominate their conversation.

Men usually hunt alone or in pairs, and often take along their dogs. Good hunting dogs are highly valued. Shotguns, obtained through trade, have largely replaced the bow and arrow. The use of guns has cut down on the number of animals in the forest. Blowguns are still used to hunt birds and monkeys because the silent darts do not scare away the game. The Barasana also hunt tapirs, armadillos, and peccaries. They go after specific animals but will take anything they come across.

As hunters walk through the forest they are continually on the lookout for any food that can be gathered. In the rainy season, large quantities of forest fruits are collected. Ants, caterpillars, frogs, and grubs are eaten. Smoked fish and meat and other foods are stored for exchanging with other malocas during dances.

Hunting weapons
Blowguns are made from two hollow tubes of palm wood with a hardwood mouthpiece. Darts and hunting arrows are tipped with poison.

Blowgun

Dart

Outer tube

Hardwood mouthpiece

Quiver for darts

Bow and arrows

Section through blowgun showing inner tube

Forest game

Woolly monkey
Monkeys are called by making sucking noises with cupped hands, then shot with blowguns.

Toucan
Hunters imitate the toucan's call to lure them. Their bright feathers are used for ornaments.

Peccary
These piglike animals are shot with guns or arrows, or they are trapped in hollow logs.

19

Family life

The Barasana marry partners from other Indian groups that speak different languages from their own. Children are taught to speak their father's language but know their mother's perfectly too. Adults always speak their own language but have no difficulty in understanding each other. When he marries, a young man builds a compartment inside the maloca. When a child is born, the father must stay with his wife in the compartment for ten days, fasting and avoiding all work.

Small children spend much of their time playing with other children of the maloca while older children, especially older sisters, look after them. They learn by playing together and working with their parents rather than by going to school. By the time they are six, young girls begin to help their mothers. Boys are more carefree, swimming in the rivers and bringing home small animals and fish they have caught for their mothers to cook.

For peace and privacy, families go inside their compartments in the maloca. Here, they keep fish and meat on a rack above the fire for small meals. Clothes are hung from the rafters, and the best pots and gourds are also kept in the private compartments, and men keep their fishing gear and weapons stuck in the thatch of the roof.

Women often go to visit their parents with their husbands and children. At sunrise and dusk, men sit out in the yard talking to their wives and playing with their children.

Sleeping in hammocks
Family members sleep in hammocks inside their own compartment. Hammocks made from palm leaf fiber were invented by the Indians, but many now prefer cotton hammocks bought from traders.

21

A man's life

Coca leaves
Chewing coca is an important ritual of the Barasana men.

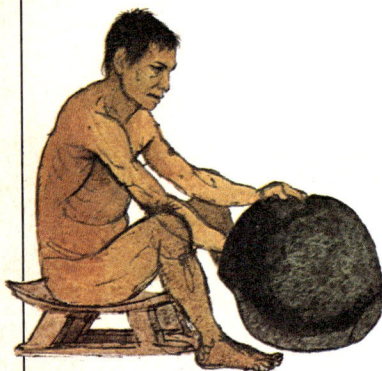

Preparing coca
Coca leaves are toasted in a pot and then pounded in a mortar to make a fine powder.

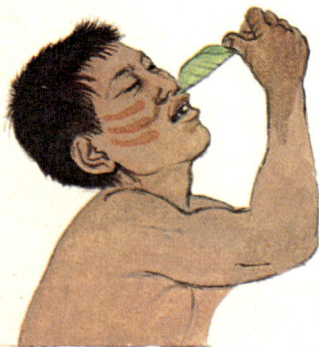

Chili pepper juice
Juice from crushed peppers is inhaled to purify the body and the spirit.

In the past the Barasana were brave warriors. They fought with strangers in distant malocas and later with the rubber gatherers who tried to force the Indians to work for them. Today there is no more warfare, but men who are especially brave and tough are still much admired.

When young men come of age and are initiated, they are whipped and given magical things to eat to make them strong. They show off their skill at hunting, chopping down trees, paddling canoes, and dancing.

After marriage, men make gardens for their wives, and hunt and fish to feed their families. Every night the men sit together in the middle of the maloca discussing the day's events. The headman encourages his brothers to work together but he cannot give them orders.

The men spend much of their time growing and preparing coca. (Coca is also the plant from which the drug cocaine is made.) Other crops grown by men— tobacco, and corn for making beer—are also used during rituals when outsiders come to dance and the men make contact with the spirit world.

Men who are good hunters and have many visitors earn the respect of the other Indians. They clear large gardens so that they will have plenty of manioc and maize to make beer, and plenty of coca to give their guests.

Basket making
Although baskets are used by women, only men are allowed to make them. Young men are taught to weave baskets as part of their initiation.

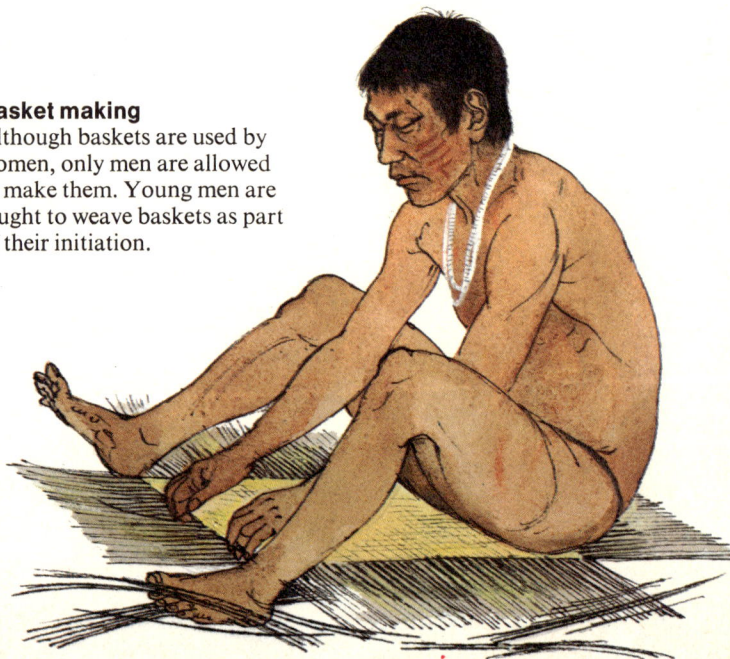

Initiation

When boys approach adolescence, they go through an initiation rite. They decorate their bodies with beads and paint and are shown sacred flutes and trumpets which women and younger children are forbidden to see. While the adults play the flutes, the young men are given yagé— a drink that makes them see visions.

The shaman

Shamans act as priests and doctors. Some of them are believed to be able to cure illness, which, according to the Indians, is caused by spirits. The shaman sits his patient on a stool and rubs his hands over the sick person. When he has located the affected part he sucks hard. Then the shaman spits out animal fur or spines, which he says have caused the illness.

Myth and magic

The Indians' beliefs are based on myths about the beginning of time. They believe that the sun made the world in the form of a big maloca. In the beginning there were no people. The first ancestors, the sun's children, came into the world through the front door in the east. They swam west in the form of anacondas (water snakes).

When they got to the Pirá-Paraná region, the anacondas stopped and turned into people. Each anaconda made people who spoke a different language. These first people had names like Tapir, Jaguar, Armadillo, and Deer, the names of the forest animals. At first people and animals were like each other and lived in the same way. But as people learned to use fire for cooking and for burning the forest, and as they learned to make gardens, build houses, and live together, they became different from animals.

When the first people died their bones are said to have turned into the sacred trumpets used at initiation rites. Their souls became spirit animals in the forest. Today when people die, they float down the underworld river to the west. Their souls join the animals and ancestors in the forest, and then return as newborn babies.

In the old days, when a person died, a ceremony was held at which masks representing all the animals of the forest were worn. These were spirit animals welcoming the soul of the dead person back into their world.

Since Indians believe that animals and people were the same in the past and that animals and spirits live together today, to go hunting is like going to war. When animals are killed, their spirits try to take revenge. Through their meat, they try to send magic darts into the bodies of the hunter and his family, causing them to become ill. Shamans blow magic spells over the meat to make it safe to eat.

When the souls of the dead return from the spirit world as babies, they are given the names of dead grandparents. Mothers have their babies in the gardens outside the maloca and bring them in through the back door, the door in the west. When a baby is born the spirits are jealous and try to get its soul back. The spirits try to kill the baby, and the shaman, who is thought to be in touch with the spirit world, must make magic spells to protect the newborn child.

Rock carvings
Strange figures and patterns are carved in the rocks of the Pirá-Paraná. The Indians believe they were made by the first ancestors when they paused to dance and sing on their journey upriver. The one above is thought to represent the river god, Ni. Ni is said to dwell in a palace in an underwater cave below the rapids, singing to the drawings and the spirits.

25

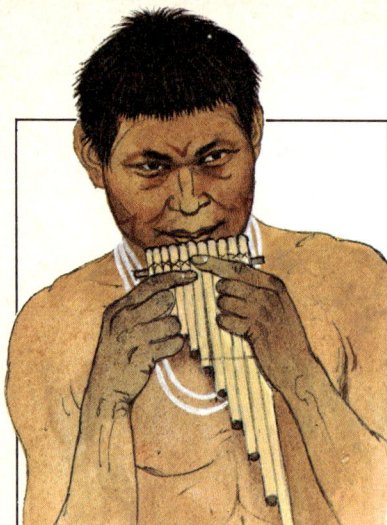

Panpipes
Teams of young men dance as they play on pipes made from hollow reeds bound together.

Gatherings

Indians travel a great deal and rely on each other for hospitality. It is an unusual week in a maloca when someone does not arrive for a visit. The Indians go to visit relatives, to trade, or to seek help. But when they invite guests to their own maloca it is always to dance and drink beer. There are many different kinds of ritual festivals held throughout the year. Guests sometimes bring huge quantities of smoked fish and meat, or baskets of forest fruit.

On the day before a dance, women gather manioc and other roots. Boiled roots and toasted manioc bread are chewed and then put in a trough with juice to make beer. Men pick coca leaves and grind them into powder. The house is swept clean and the earth floor is sprinkled with water to keep down the dust. Young men practice on reed pipes and elders get costumes ready for the dance.

Dances are important events to people living in isolated malocas in the forest, and these gatherings serve many purposes. They are religious rituals, a time for fun and visiting, an opportunity to exchange news and goods, and a chance to make new friends.

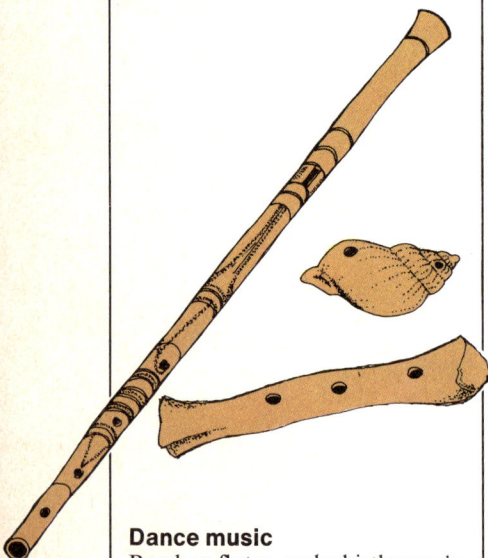

Dance music
Bamboo flutes, and whistles made of shell and bone are played at dances to waken yagé spirits. Ankle rattles of fruit husks lend rhythm to the music.

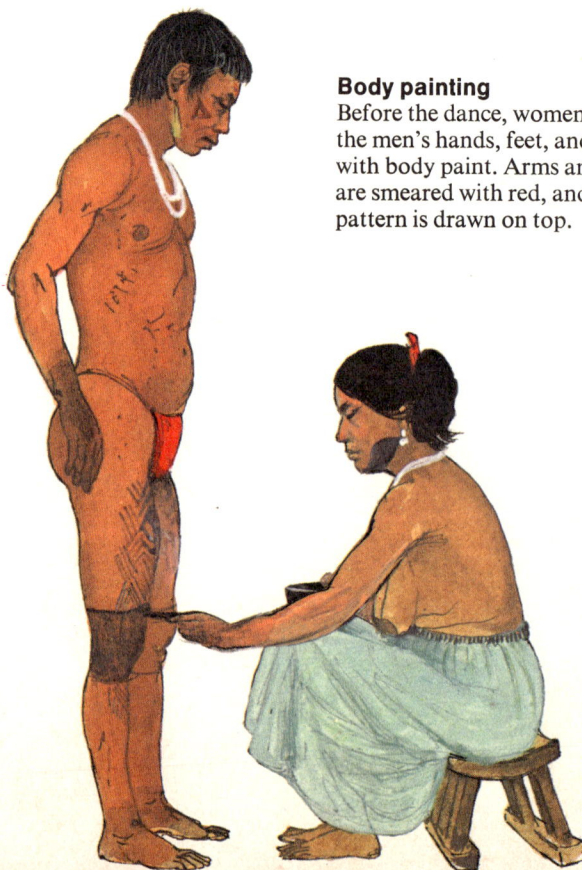

Body painting
Before the dance, women blacken the men's hands, feet, and knees with body paint. Arms and legs are smeared with red, and a black pattern is drawn on top.

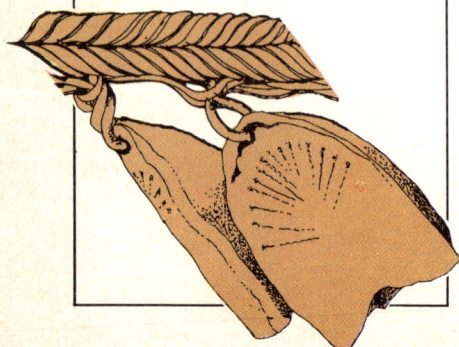

Dancing costume

Ritual ornaments have magic power and only men may wear them. They are the dress of spirits and ancestors. A dancer wears a feather crown with egret plumes at the back. Around his neck is a quartz ornament. His belt is of peccary or jaguar teeth. He wears a painted bark-cloth apron with sweet-smelling leaves tucked under his belt at the back. Below his knees are woven garters and he has a rattle on one ankle and a band of white bark on the other.

Egret plumes

Feather and down headdress

Macaw tail-feather

Jaguar-bone support

Brass ear pendant

White quartz pendant

Arm beads

Belt of jaguar teeth

Bark-cloth apron

Sweet-smelling leaves

Painted baton

Garters

Body paint

Ankle rattles

Yagé pot

A brightly-painted pot holds yagé, made from the bark of a vine, pounded and mixed with water. The bitter yagé liquid, served at dances, gives visions of the spirit world.

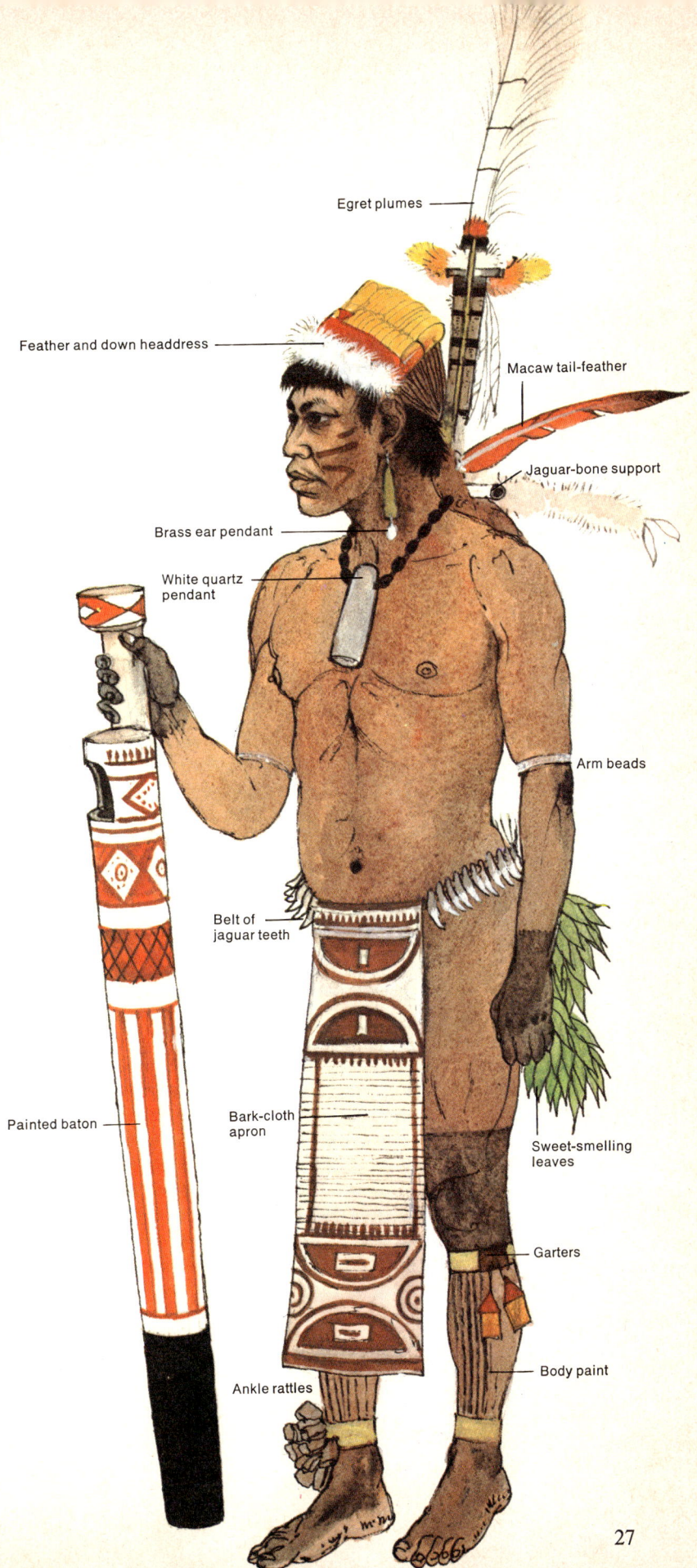

Drinking and dancing

Dances usually start in the morning and continue without a break until the next day. The guests arrive by canoe or on foot, stopping at the river bank to bathe and decorate themselves. The men go in at the front of the house, chanting loud greetings. The women, loaded down with baskets and with babies on their hips, go in at the back.

The visitors are served gourds of beer, which they must drink in one gulp. The men prepare for dancing, putting on their headdresses and ornaments, and shaking rattles and gourds. As one group dances in a line, reed pipes are played in chorus. The young men spring up, weaving in and out of the houseposts, playing their pipes and taking girls by the hand to dance.

When there is a break in the dancing, the men sit in a circle drinking yagé and chanting the myths of their ancestors. In their yagé visions, the men see the maloca as the universe, filled with ancestral spirits dressed in feathers and paint.

At the end of the dance, everyone is tired and happy. The shaman removes the men's headdresses, blowing spells to protect them from the danger of wearing sacred things. The people go down to the river to bathe, then return to their hammocks to sleep through the day. At dusk a big meal is served, the first since the dancing began. The next day, the visitors drift home carrying gifts of food from their relatives and goods traded with other people.

An uncertain future

The Indians of the Vaupés are not yet an endangered species. But the old ways still followed by the Barasana have largely disappeared in the region except on isolated rivers like the Pirá-Paraná. The malocas have gone, and with them the values that gave meaning to life in the forest. Most Indians now live in villages on the river banks. Each family has its own house with clay walls and a thatched roof. On the Pirá-Paraná there is still plenty to eat, but elsewhere the diet is poor.

Missionaries have urged the Indians to live in villages. Here they receive good educations but not without losing in other ways. Children go to boarding schools instead of learning to live in the forest. They learn about the outside world—about cities and towns and automobiles—instead of being taught their own culture by their parents. When they go back to their homes they are unsuited to the old life and cut off from the new.

It is easy to see the problems facing the Indians, but it is not so easy to solve them. Giving Indians rights to the lands where they live might help them to go on feeding themselves. But the Indians have become used to using steel axes and machetes (introduced by traders) and their life would now be nearly impossible without them. They need money to buy these goods, and ways to earn money are difficult to find.

The rubber industry used Indians as laborers early in this century (and killed many of them by exposing them to disease). But now it is cheaper to manufacture imitation rubber than to tap the rubber trees of the Amazon. Hunting jaguars for their skins has been outlawed. It is nearly impossible to make a living by selling fruits and vegetables in the towns, and laborers' jobs are scarce.

New roads, which are being built into the area from Brazil, may make it possible for the Indians to sell their produce and handicrafts in distant cities. But improved roads may also bring settlers to take away the land and cut down the forest on which the Indians' lives depend.

Although they live much as their ancestors did, the Indians of the Vaupés have adapted to the presence of new people; they are open and curious about the outside world. But until they can find a way to fit into Colombian and Brazilian society, their future remains uncertain.

Index